OPRAH WINFREY

SUCCESS WITH AN OPEN HEART

Tanya Lee Stone

A GATEWAY BIOGRAPHY

THE MILLBROOK PRESS

BROOKFIELD, CONNECTICUT

For Jake, *my* "talkingest" child.

Published by The Millbrook Press, Inc.
2 Old New Milford Road
Brookfield, Connecticut 06804

Library of Congress Cataloging-in-Publication Data
Stone, Tanya Lee.
Oprah Winfrey: success with an open heart / Tanya Lee Stone.
p. cm.
Includes index.
ISBN 0-7613-1814-3 (lib. bdg.)
1. Winfrey, Oprah—Juvenile literature. 2. Television personalities—United
States—Biography—Juvenile literature. 3. Motion picture actors and
actresses—United States—Biography—Juvenile literature. [1. Winfrey,
Oprah. 2. Television personalities. 3. Actors and actresses.
4. Women—Biography. 5. Afro-Americans—Biography.] I. Title.
PN1992.40.W56   S76   2001
791.45'028'092—dc21
[B]   00-41116

Cover photograph courtesy of © Evan Agostini/Liaison Agency
Photographs courtesy of Liaison Agency: pp. 4 (© Arnaldo Magnani), 20
(© Lawrence Schwartzwald), 27 (© James Schnepf), 31 (© Cynthia
Johnson), 35 (© Arnald Magnani), 39 (© Evan Agostini); Metropolitan
Government Archives, Nashville/Davidson County Tennessee: p. 9;
Classmates.com Yearbook Archives: pp. 13, 14; *The Tennessean*: p. 16;
The Metropolitan Times: p. 17; Photofest: pp. 23, 28, 33 (bottom);
Archive Photos: pp. 25 (© Victor Malafronte), 30 (© Victor Malafronte),
33 (top: © Reuters/Gregory Heisler); Corbis/Sygma: pp. 37 (© Bob
Daemmrich), 38 (© Henry Bargas), 40 (© Gregory Pace)

OPRAH WINFREY

Oprah Winfrey
IS ONE OF THE MOST
RECOGNIZABLE
WOMEN IN SHOW
BUSINESS.

In 1997, Oprah Winfrey had a decision to make. She had been hosting an award-winning television show for eleven years. She was both physically and mentally tired and wasn't sure she wanted to keep the show going. People were saying that Oprah was going to give up. But instead of quitting, Oprah decided to change her show to make it better—for herself and for her audience. She thought about the great gift of success she had been given. And she wondered how she could make what millions of people saw on *The Oprah Winfrey Show* more meaningful.

Oprah decided it was time to create what she calls "Change Your Life TV." She began to focus on helping people lead happier lives. By watching the Oprah show, people can learn to understand themselves better and work on changing bad habits that have made them unhappy.

One of the things that helped Oprah make up her mind to continue her show was her own heritage. As an African-

American woman, she says, "I realized that I had no right to quit, coming from a history of people who had no voice, who had no power, and that I have been given this . . . blessed opportunity to speak to people, to . . . make a difference in their lives."

Oprah Winfrey is certainly no quitter. From the very beginning of her life, she has had hard things to overcome. And from the beginning, she worked hard, held her head high, and made it through.

It was January 29, 1954. In a small farmhouse in the rolling hills of Mississippi, an eighteen-year-old named Vernita Lee gave birth to a baby girl. The baby was to be named after a woman in the Bible called Orpah. But there was a spelling mistake in the birth record, and the "r" and "p" were switched. The baby who was born that day has been known as Oprah Gail ever since.

Oprah's father, Vernon Winfrey, was twenty years old when she was born. Vernon and Vernita were not married. Vernon was in the military, and Vernita was young, poor, and scared. After a few years, Vernita decided that she could not take care of her small daughter. Vernita asked her mother, Hattie Mae Lee, to care for Oprah. Then Vernita got on a Greyhound bus and moved to Milwaukee.

Oprah spent the next two years living with her grandmother Hattie Mae and her grandfather Earless (Ur-liss).

They lived on a farm outside of Kosciusko, Mississippi. Oprah's grandparents raised chickens, turkeys, pigs, and cows. They also had a vegetable garden and grew most of what they ate. Oprah learned to help take care of the animals and fetch water from the well.

There was no bathroom in the house, no radio, and no television. Oprah did not have her own room and owned only two pairs of shoes. Since she had to keep them clean for church, she often ran barefoot around the farm. Hattie Mae was very strict and Oprah was hit if she did not do as she was told.

But there were good things about living with Hattie Mae, too. It was her grandmother who encouraged Oprah to read—something that would always be a very important part of her life. By the time Oprah was three, Hattie Mae had also taught her to add, subtract, and write. In church, the young Oprah liked to read aloud. She was very good at it and made Hattie Mae proud. The other women at the church would say, "Hattie Mae, this child is gifted," and "This child sure can talk. She is the *talkingest* child."

Oprah has said about Hattie Mae, "I am what I am because of my grandmother; my strength, my sense of reasoning, everything. All of that was set by the time I was six years old. I basically am no different now from what I was when I was six."

Still, Oprah knew she wanted a different life for herself from the one she lived on her grandmother's farm. "I remember standing on the back porch looking through the screen. My grandmother was boiling clothes [to get them clean] and saying, 'Watch this because one day you're going to have to learn how to do this.' And I remember thinking, 'No, I'm not.'"

In 1960, when Oprah was six years old, her grandmother became ill. Oprah was sent to Milwaukee to be with her mother. Vernita had a job and was planning to get married, so she thought things would be fine. But when Oprah got to Milwaukee, she found out that she had a half sister named Patricia. Right away, the two girls did not get along. Oprah was given a cot on the porch. She felt sad and lonely.

Within two years, Vernita realized that she couldn't take care of her children as well as she had hoped to. She had not gotten married and the family was living in one room in a crowded boardinghouse in downtown Milwaukee. This time, Vernita asked for help from Oprah's father, Vernon.

Vernon was happy to have Oprah live with him and his wife, Zelma. Oprah was just starting third grade when she moved to Nashville, Tennessee, to live with the Winfreys. Oprah loved to read and was very smart. And even though she had skipped from kindergarten to second grade within a few weeks, her mother had not encouraged her. It was much different with Zelma. Zelma was strict about schoolwork and also tutored Oprah at home. Oprah remembers, "I had to do book reports at home as well as in school and so many vocabulary words a week." Oprah also found support from a teacher named Mary Duncan. Oprah says, "I wasn't afraid to be smart in Miss Duncan's class and she encouraged me to read as much as I could, and she would stay after school with me."

At the end of the school year, Oprah went to Milwaukee to spend the summer vacation with her mother. But when it came time for Oprah to go home to Nashville, Vernita said no. Her mother planned to marry and wanted her family back together. Vernita gave birth to a baby boy named Jeffrey, but she did not get married. Instead, she and her children all moved into a two-bedroom apartment. Oprah missed the life she had with her father. The next few years in Milwaukee were very hard for her.

Vernita had friends and relatives drifting in and out of their apartment. Oprah often didn't feel safe. She felt unloved by her mother and she and her sister, Patricia, fought a lot. And when Oprah was just nine years old, a nineteen-year-old cousin sexually abused her and told her not to tell anyone. Life at home for Oprah was very unhappy. She became so angry that she ran away from home more than once. Things weren't much better at school. She

OPRAH'S FATHER, VERNON WINFREY, WAS A STRICT BUT LOVING PARENT. LIVING WITH HIM HELPED OPRAH TO GROW UP RIGHT. THIS PICTURE OF VERNON WAS TAKEN IN 1975.

was smarter than many of the students at the rough Lincoln School she went to, and the other kids picked on her. They called her "the Preacher" because she was so good at public speaking. They often threatened to beat her up.

One of Oprah's teachers at Lincoln School, Gene Abrams, noticed that Oprah always sat alone reading a book during free time at school. After finding out what a smart and promising student she was, he arranged for her to go to a better school. At the time, Oprah was one of only a few black students at her new school—Nicolet High School in a Milwaukee suburb called Fox Point. She later said that Mr. Abrams was "one of those great teachers who had the ability to make you believe in yourself."

For Oprah, Nicolet was a whole new world. Each day, the fourteen-year-old took several different buses over twenty miles each way just to get to school. Most of the students came from white, upper-class families that did not seem to have any of the problems Oprah had known. "The life that I saw those children lead was so totally different from what I went home to, from what I saw when I took the bus home with the maids in the evening. I wanted my mother to be like their mothers. I wanted my mother to have cookies ready for me when I came home and to say, 'How was your day?'" As a grown-up, Oprah came to understand that her mother had done the best she could. But at the time, returning home from Nicolet at the end of the day "was like going back to Cinderella's house from the castle every night."

Even though Oprah loved school, she was getting into more and more trouble. She had also suffered more sexual abuse. The pressure to keep up with her classmates who could afford things Oprah could not caused her to steal. One time she even faked a robbery at her house to cover up for the things she had taken from her mother. She would also lie, saying she was going to a friend's house and then staying out all night. Oprah has said, "After seeing how the other half lived, I started having some real problems. I guess you could call me *troubled*—to put it mildly." The last straw came when Oprah was returned home after running away. Her mother, tired of taking care of her difficult daughter, tried to put Oprah in a home for girls with problems. Thankfully for Oprah, there was no room for her there and she was sent to live with her father again.

And again, life at her father's house was much different from life at her mother's. Vernon and Zelma Winfrey gave her a safe and loving place to live. But Oprah had gone back to the Winfreys with a secret. At the age of fourteen, Oprah was pregnant. The baby, however, did not survive.

To help Oprah stay out of trouble, Zelma and Vernon took good care of her. They did not let her stay out late, wear skimpy clothes, or break their rules. Oprah later said, "When my father took me in, it changed...my life. He saved me." She also said, "I knew that I couldn't get away with [anything] anymore. So I settled down and never pulled another trick." And once again, Zelma encouraged Oprah to read. In no time, Zelma had her stepdaughter reading up to five books every two weeks.

When Oprah started at Nashville's East High School in 1968, black and white students were just starting to go to the same schools together. Sometimes it was hard for everyone to get along. But Oprah was popular and was good at bringing both black and white students together even when things got tense. She was happier than she had ever been. She even fell in love for the first time, with a boy named Anthony Otey. Oprah and Anthony took walks in the park, ate hamburgers, went to the movies, and listened to music. In her senior year, Oprah was elected president of the student council. She was also chosen "Most Popular Girl." Anthony was picked as "Most Popular Boy."

Oprah easily got A's in school. As she had when she was three years old and living with her grandmother, Oprah started speaking to church groups. She was such a great speaker that people from many different churches started to ask for her. She also often won speaking contests. One of her high school friends, Luvenia Harrison Butler, said, "I remember Oprah always coming back with the trophy. . . . Our high school was always winning because she was so good."

Oprah liked to speak about slavery and the rights of both women and African Americans. When she was seventeen, Oprah was invited to a White House Conference on Youth and entered a national speaking contest. A year earlier, she had been asked to speak to a church group in Los Angeles,

OPRAH WAS VOTED "MOST POPULAR GIRL" IN HER HIGH SCHOOL YEARBOOK, AND HER THEN-BOYFRIEND, ANTHONY (SEATED NEXT TO HER), WAS VOTED "MOST POPULAR BOY."

OPRAH PRACTICED HER PUBLIC-SPEAKING SKILLS IN
A SCHOOL CLUB IN ADDITION TO THE PRACTICE SHE GOT
SPEAKING AT CHURCHES. SHE IS IN THE LOWER-LEFT-HAND
CORNER OF THE PICTURE.

California. While she was there, she fell in love with Hollywood. Oprah knew then that she wanted to be in the spotlight. And it wouldn't be long before her dream of becoming a star would come true.

In her senior year, Oprah took part in a walk to raise money for the March of Dimes Birth Defects Foundation. (This organization works to improve the health of babies by preventing birth defects.) One of the people she asked to sponsor her was a disc jockey at WVOL, a radio station near where she lived in Nashville. The station's general manager, Clarence Kilcrease, heard her talk and thought Oprah had a wonderful speaking voice. He asked her to talk on the radio. Soon, she was reading the news after school and getting paid $100 a week!

Oprah had a great style on the air and became very popular. The radio station asked her to enter a beauty contest for them called Miss Fire Prevention. "I know it's not a biggie, but I was the only black—the first black—to win the darned thing," she remembers. She went on to win other beauty and talent contests, including Miss Black Nashville and Miss Black Tennessee. The most important prize she won was four years of college at Tennessee State University in Nashville, paid for by a scholarship.

By the time she graduated from high school in 1971, Oprah had lived up to one of her favorite sayings, "Bloom where you are planted." She had changed from an unhappy, troubled girl into a young woman with growing confidence.

OPRAH AS
"MISS BLACK
NASHVILLE"

ollege offered Oprah new challenges. She studied drama and speech. And even though she did well in her classes and made some friends, college life was not easy. Tennessee State was an all-black college and many students were angry about civil rights. She has said, "It was a weird time. This whole black power movement was going on then, but I just never had any of those angry black feelings. . . . I hated, hated, hated college." Oprah spent all her time on her studies and her work at the radio station.

She went to class in the morning and worked at WVOL in the afternoon. She loved working at the radio station and was learning a lot and becoming very good at it. Then, in her second year of college, WTVF-TV, a local television station, wanted her to come there and be the anchorperson on their news broadcast. She auditioned and was offered the job. She struggled with the decision of taking the job because it meant leaving college. But finally she decided to take it. With that, Oprah became an anchorwoman at age nineteen and the first black

OPRAH ENJOYED HER JOB READING THE NEWS ON THE AIR AT RADIO STATION WVOL IN NASHVILLE.

woman to read the news on television in Nashville. She worked at WTVF for three years.

In the early 1970s, women and minorities were just starting to be hired for broadcast jobs that had usually been given to white men in the past. Oprah's natural talent, helped by the fact that she was both female and black, landed her a great job in 1976. She was offered a chance to do the evening news for a major television station, WJZ, in Baltimore, Maryland. Oprah moved out of her father's house and went to Baltimore. She was twenty-two years old and on her way. But things did not go as smoothly as she had hoped.

From the start, Oprah and the other news anchor, Jerry Turner, did not work well on the air together. Turner was a polished, respected news anchor and he made the inexperienced Oprah feel stiff and nervous. Oprah also had trouble reading sad news because she cared so much about what happened to people. Instead of simply reporting a story of a fire or a crime, she would get upset on the air. She also spent time trying to help the victims of several of the crimes she was reporting. Oprah remembers, "I really wasn't cut out for the news. I'd have to fight back the tears if a story was too sad." And, she added, "It was not good for a news reporter to be out covering a fire and crying with a woman who has lost her home." The news director was not happy with Oprah. After nine months of trying her best, the anchor job was given to someone else and Oprah was given smaller reporting jobs to do instead.

WJZ also tried to change the way Oprah looked by giving her a makeover. It was a disaster. She was given a bad hairstyle at a fancy salon. A shaky Oprah didn't stand up for herself at the time. Looking back on the experience, Oprah says she learned a valuable lesson. "What I should have said then, and what I would say now, is that nobody can tell me how to wear my hair. I've since vowed to live my own life, to always be myself." But at the time, she was losing her confidence.

One bright spot was that Oprah had made an important friend at WJZ, a woman named Gayle King. Gayle was also working on her television career. One night during a bad snowstorm Oprah told Gayle that she could sleep at her house because Oprah lived closer to work. The two young women stayed up all night talking. More than twenty years later Oprah said, "Ever since then, we talk every day, sometimes three or four times." And like a true best friend, Gayle says, "I tell her everything. There are things that Oprah knows that nobody else does." Having a friend like Gayle made a huge difference in Oprah's life.

A change at the station was about to help Oprah, too. In 1977, the station hired a new manager, Bill Baker. He knew that Oprah had special talents and that she should be doing something more than reporting. Baker also knew that he wanted to create a talk show that could compete with the popular *Phil Donahue Show*. He asked Oprah Winfrey and another talented person at the station—Richard Sher—to co-host a new morning show called *People Are Talking*. The very

ALTHOUGH AT FIRST OPRAH DID NOT ENJOY HER JOB AT TELEVISION STATION WJZ, SHE WAS LUCKY ENOUGH TO MEET GAYLE KING, WHO BECAME HER BEST FRIEND AND EVENTUALLY A BUSINESS PARTNER. THIS PICTURE OF OPRAH AND GAYLE (LEFT) WAS TAKEN IN 1999.

first day changed Oprah's life forever. "I finished that [first] show, and I thought, 'This is it. This is what I was born to do. This is like breathing.'"

Oprah cohosted *People Are Talking* until 1983. The show was very popular and Oprah got better every year. She was warm and friendly, and people trusted her. She asked good questions and really listened to people's answers. She seemed to be everyone's understanding friend. And although she and her cohost worked very well together, Oprah also learned that she wanted to have a show of her own. After a while, it was time for her to go. "When you have finished growing in one place or time, you know. Your soul tells you when it's time to move on," said Oprah.

Oprah did move on. In September 1983, she went to Chicago. One of the women who had worked on *People Are Talking*, Debra DiMaio, had taken a job on a show called *A.M. Chicago* at WLS-TV. When that show needed a new host, DiMaio told her boss that Oprah would be a great choice. Oprah auditioned for station manager Dennis Swanson and got the job. It was this next step in her career that would lead to Oprah's fame.

Her first show aired on January 2, 1984. She was nervous and wasn't sure if a black female television host would be welcomed in Chicago. But she also knew that Chicago felt like home. Oprah had nothing to worry about. She was a hit. She loved Chicago—and Chicago loved her. She says, "I'll never leave Chicago, the best city in the world."

Oprah's style of simply being herself on the air made people open up to her. She liked to ask celebrities questions that the average fan might want to know. She also wanted to interview ordinary people and talk about subjects that affect everybody. And she shared difficult and personal stories from her own life. Her staff soon learned that it was best not to write Oprah's questions for her. Instead, she was given some background information about a guest and Oprah would take the interview from there.

Within just three months, Oprah had won over the local audience. People started watching Oprah Winfrey instead of Phil Donahue. Since Donahue had hosted the most popular talk show in Chicago for sixteen years, that was big news. Within seven months, the show was expanded from thirty minutes to an hour. Oprah chose the guests and picked the topics. By the end of 1984, *Newsweek* magazine called her the "hottest press star in Chicago" and guessed that soon she would be known all over the country.

Newsweek was right. Oprah made *A.M. Chicago* so popular that in just three years it was being broadcast not just in the Chicago area but all over America. On September 8, 1986, the renamed *Oprah Winfrey Show* aired on 138 stations throughout the nation. She soon had an audience of more than ten million viewers. In the process, Oprah became a multimillionaire.

As amazing as that success was, another of Oprah's dreams had come true the year before—the dream of becoming an actress.

In December 1984, entertainment producer Quincy Jones was on a visit to Chicago. Watching television in his hotel room, he saw Oprah on her talk show. Right away, Jones knew she would be perfect for the role of Sofia in a movie he was making with director Steven Spielberg. The movie was *The Color Purple*, based on a book by Alice Walker. The book had been a favorite of Oprah's since it was published in 1982. In fact, she loved it so much that she always had a copy of it with her and she had written a letter to Walker, asking the author to let her know if there would ever be a chance to make a movie about the book!

OPRAH AS SOFIA IN THE COLOR PURPLE

When Oprah found out about Jones's interest in her, she could hardly believe it. "Quincy Jones was in Chicago for six hours—six hours! And he turned on the TV set and saw me, and said, 'There's Sofia.' And he didn't even know if I could act!" She flew to Hollywood to audition for the part—and she got it. She was given twelve weeks off from her show to do the movie. *The Color Purple* opened on December 18, 1985. Oprah Winfrey received an Academy Award nomination for Best Supporting Actress. She had gotten national attention as an actress and her popularity was about to skyrocket.

prah knew it was her time to shine. "I intend to do and have it all. I want to have a movie career, a television career, a talk-show career." Oprah had blossomed into a totally confident woman. "I believe in my own possibilities and I feel I can do it all," she said.

In 1986, the year that *The Oprah Winfrey Show* went national, Oprah fell in love with Stedman Graham Jr., a businessman who also founded and ran a program called Athletes Against Drugs. The tall, handsome Graham seemed to be the perfect match for Oprah. She calls him "six-feet-six of terrific." That year Oprah also made another movie. This time she had a major role in *Native Son*, based on the book by Richard Wright. The movie deals with racism and violence. Oprah played the mother of an angry African-American man who

Oprah and
Stedman Graham
in 1998

Oprah became a huge celebrity in 1986. She was getting thousands of fan letters every week and making guest appearances all over the country. As Oprah's fame grew, people started to see what her friends had long known—that she is very generous. She shares her good fortune with the people in her life and reaches out to many who are less fortunate. In 1986, Oprah started a Big Sisters group at the Cabrini-Green housing project in Chicago. In 1987, she paid for ten scholarships to Tennessee State University in her father's name. Each year, she adds money to that cause. In 1989, she gave $1 million to Morehouse College in Atlanta, Georgia. And in 1991, Oprah gave $100,000 to a new Chicago library because of her love for books. These are just a few examples of Oprah's giving spirit. That spirit seems to grow more and more as time goes on.

commits a crime. The following year, in 1987, Oprah made show business history. With her fame and wealth, she was able to do something that only two women before her—Lucille Ball and Mary Pickford—had done, and she was the first black woman to do so: Oprah Winfrey opened her own studio to produce movies and television shows. She named it Harpo, which is "Oprah" spelled backward. Harpo also happens to be the name of Sofia's husband in *The Color Purple*.

Oprah added another first to her list in 1987: She won an Emmy award for Outstanding Talk Show Host and one for Outstanding Talk Show. Oprah has gone on to win seven more Emmys for Outstanding Host and nine more for Outstanding Show. That same year, she was named Female Star of the Year and received the Golden Apple Award from the Hollywood Women's Press Club.

In 1988, Harpo bought *The Oprah Winfrey Show,* which had been owned by ABC and WLS. This made her even richer and gave Oprah the control she was looking for. She was now working for herself and could do what she wanted. She said, "I just want to do good work, so I have created an environment for that." She also made Harpo a place where people felt at home. "I wanted to create a place . . . where people respected one another and were friendly and were also friends," she said.

OPRAH WORKS ON IDEAS FOR HER SHOW WITH JEFFREY JACOBS, PRESIDENT OF HARPO.

O**PRAH** (RIGHT) DANCES IN THE STREET IN A SCENE FROM T**HE** W**OMEN** OF B**REWSTER** P**LACE**.

The first movie that Harpo worked on was for television. It was called *The Women of Brewster Place*. Oprah was again able to play a role that she deeply believed in. She played Mattie Michael, a strong woman who gave her wisdom and support to the other women in the made-up town of Brewster Place. The movie was aired in March 1989. That same year, Oprah herself was recognized as a strong woman. *Ms.* magazine chose her for one of its Woman of the Year Awards.

After *Brewster Place*, Harpo began work on more movies. Oprah opened a restaurant in Chicago called the Eccentric. And the daily talk show went on. In 1991, Oprah also started working on afterschool specials with ABC. They focused on teen issues such as self-esteem, racial tensions, and drugs.

Something else happened around this time that touched Oprah deeply. After doing a show about child abuse and hearing a related news story that made her sad, she decided it was time to do more. Oprah asked former Illinois Governor James Thompson to write a law to protect children. The goal was to create a national registry of child abusers. Employers and people who work with children could use the registry in order to avoid hiring people who are dangerous to children. On November 12, 1991, Oprah spoke to lawmakers in

In 1988, while making Brewster Place *and keeping up with her daily show, Oprah lost a lot of weight on a strict diet. She has struggled her whole life with her weight and was very proud of getting thin. Her weight has gone up and down since then, but she has stopped trying to lose weight with diets that may not be healthy. Instead, she has learned to focus on feeling good about her body, exercising, and eating right.*

Oprah's best friend, Gayle, has noticed the difference in Oprah's eating habits. In 1994, Gayle said, "She can eat a muffin without butter and say it tastes good." Oprah even ran a marathon that year. She said, "It's the best feeling I have ever had, actually. . . .This is the first time I ever really set a goal and had to work this hard to get to it." And in 1995, Oprah and her trainer Bob Greene got many Americans exercising with the "Get Movin' with Oprah" program. Oprah and Greene created a nutrition and exercise section for the show that ran for six weeks. She and Greene also wrote a book together on the subject of exercise and nutrition. It is called Make the Connection: Ten Steps to a Better Body—and a Better Life. *Oprah said, "We want to get the whole country involved in spring training—getting moving. Getting America walking, that's my new thing."*

"GET MOVIN' WITH OPRAH" WAS FILMED IN CENTRAL PARK IN NEW YORK CITY. WITH OPRAH ARE MARTHA STEWART (LEFT) AND DONNA GIULIANI (RIGHT), THE WIFE OF THE MAYOR OF NEW YORK CITY.

Washington, D.C., to help pass the National Child Protection Act. Unfortunately, at that time the law was not passed.

But Oprah didn't give up. She decided to help a filmmaker named Arnold Shapiro make a movie called *Scared Silent: Exposing and Ending Child Abuse.* Oprah was the host and introduced the show by saying, "I'm Oprah Winfrey, and like millions of other Americans, I'm a survivor of child abuse." The film was shown on ABC, CBS, NBC, and PBS and received a lot of attention. Finally, on December 20, 1993, President Bill Clinton signed the National Child Protection Act into law. Oprah Winfrey was at the White House that day to watch it happen.

Oprah and others watch as President Bill Clinton signs the National Child Protection Act into law.

O prah's schedule is always very busy and she likes it that way. She finds time to do her show, be active in causes she believes in, and make films close to her heart. In 1995, Harpo Productions teamed up with Disney to make movies together. Oprah was thrilled to work with a company that she respects. She said she looked forward to making "Anything that shows the possibilities of what a human being can do and the human spirit can achieve."

Two years earlier, in 1993, Oprah had played LaJoe Rivers in *There Are No Children Here,* a movie for ABC television about black families living in a Chicago housing project. She earned $500,000 for the film and used the money to set up a scholarship fund for the real kids who live in that project. The film also led to a charity that Oprah and Stedman Graham set up together called Families for a Better Life.

There Are No Children Here also led to a deal with ABC to make more movies. Under the name Oprah Winfrey Presents, Oprah could choose six scripts she loved and turn them into movies. In 1997, she produced and acted in *Before Women Had Wings. The Wedding, David and Lisa,* and *Tuesdays with Morrie* all followed.

In 1998, Oprah finished a movie that had taken her more than ten years to make. She had read author Toni Morrison's book *Beloved* in 1987 and instantly knew she was meant to make it into a movie. She says, "I felt that *Beloved* was part of the reason I was born, to tell that story on screen." Oprah

OPRAH AND HER YOUNG COSTARS IN A PUBLICITY PHOTO FOR THERE ARE NO CHILDREN HERE.

DANNY GLOVER AND OPRAH IN A SCENE FROM BELOVED.

bought the film rights from Toni Morrison. In the movie, she plays Sethe, a slave who has escaped. To get ready for the part, Oprah learned a little bit about what it felt like to be Sethe. For three days, she worked in the fields and was often yelled at by actors pretending to be plantation overseers. Oprah was so thrilled on October 16, 1998, when the movie was released in theaters, that she said, "Today's the day I'm having my baby!" But the movie didn't draw crowds of people. It didn't do well. She was upset, but she recovered in true Oprah fashion. That was when she started thinking about new ways to make her talk show better.

In September 1996, she started Oprah's Book Club to get more people reading. She says, "Books opened windows to the world for me. If I can help open them for someone else, I'm happy." Eight or nine times a year, Oprah chooses a book she loves. Viewers from all over the country read the book and then share their thoughts. People respect Oprah's opinion so much that most books she chooses become national bestsellers because everyone rushes out to buy them! Oprah was even given the National Book Foundation's 50th Anniversary Gold Medal in November 1999 because she has inspired so many people to read.

Oprah's success continues to help her help others. On September 18, 1997, she announced an idea she had to make the world a better place. She started Oprah's Angel Network to bring Americans together for good causes. In its first two years, she asked viewers to send in their spare change to help

Oprah speaks after receiving her gold medal from the National Book Foundation in November 1999.

send kids to college. More than $3 million was collected and more than 150 young people were sent to college with that money. The Angel Network also helped Habitat for Humanity build nearly 200 homes for people in need. In its third year, Oprah's Angel Network decided to go wherever there was an emergency in America. It also began "The Kindness Chain," which encourages people to do something kind for someone in need. The person on the receiving end then does something kind for someone else.

Oprah finds many other ways to do her part to make the world a better place. In 1997, she made a video called *Oprah: Make the Connection.* In it, she talks about her struggle with her weight and helps people find their own ways to be healthy. Money from the sales of that video is donated to A Better Chance Program. This program has helped send inner-city kids to good private schools for thirty years. Oprah also serves as that organization's national spokesperson. And in May 2000, Oprah hosted the Chicago Black Fine Art Exposition. Money from this event was donated to Marwen, an organization that offers art education, college planning, and career development help to low-income kids.

But Oprah's fame and power have sometimes caused her trouble. In 1996, Oprah learned about mad cow disease on her show. It is an illness that cows in England had gotten that made the meat unsafe to eat. People were worried about American cows getting it. During the show, Oprah said, "It has just stopped me cold from eating another burger!" A

P EOPLE DEMONSTRATED IN TEXAS IN SUPPORT OF OPRAH AND FREE SPEECH IN 1998.

group of cattlemen from Texas got upset and said that because of Oprah's comment people weren't buying beef. They said Oprah had hurt their business and they sued her.

Oprah had to go to court in Texas to fight for her right to free speech. The first Amendment of the U.S. Constitution says, "Congress shall make no law...[restricting] the freedom of speech, or of the press..." So she took her staff to Texas and did her whole talk show from Amarillo during the trial. It was over on February 26, 1998, and Oprah had won. She said, "My reaction is free speech not only lives. It rocks."

LEAVING THE COURTHOUSE, OPRAH CELEBRATES HER VICTORY.

he fall of 1998 marked the beginning of Oprah's first season of "Change Your Life TV," a new focus for the show to keep it meaningful for herself and her viewers. She also announced that she planned to keep doing her show until 2002. Other changes were soon to follow. Harpo Entertainment Group joined other powerful women in the television business to create Oxygen Media, a new cable network and Internet company. And in April 2000, a new magazine called *O: The Oprah Magazine* hit the newsstands. Her best friend, Gayle King, is the editor-at-large. Oprah says, "This magazine provides a different way for people to be informed and inspired."

OPRAH AND HER PARTNERS AT THE LAUNCHING OF OXYGEN ON FEBRUARY 2, 2000

The first issue of O: The Oprah Magazine came out in April 2000.

Oprah Winfrey is a strong role model for all women. And she says her experience sends a special message to African-American women. Although throughout U.S. history African Americans have not had the same opportunities as whites in this country, a black woman might now look at Oprah and say, "If she can do it, I can do it." Oprah teaches all of us to live every day of our lives being true to ourselves and doing what we know in our hearts is right. She told the young women graduating from Wellesley College in 1997, "Live your life from truth and you will survive everything, everything." That is good advice for anyone, no matter their color, religion, or sex.

Everyone who knows Oprah agrees that she cares deeply for people. Talk show host Rosie O'Donnell says about Oprah, "She inspires me to reach for my better self." Gayle King says, "She really does want to help people. She really does believe that people can be better. And she really would like to be an instrument to help them get there." And even though Oprah Winfrey is one of the most powerful people in America, she is still very humble. She says, "The opportunity to have a voice and speak to the world every day is a gift. And I thank you for allowing me this gift."

Who knows what the future holds for Oprah? Her best friend, Gayle, says, "You know, Oprah's a girl who does exactly what she wants, when she wants to do it. So . . . stay tuned."

IMPORTANT DATES

January 29, 1954	Oprah Gail Winfrey is born in Mississippi.
1960	Oprah is sent to live with her mother in Milwaukee, Wisconsin.
1962	Oprah is sent to live with her father in Nashville, Tennessee.
1963	Oprah goes back to Milwaukee to live with her mother again.
1968	Oprah returns to live with her father and attends Nashville's East High School.
1971	Oprah starts college at Tennessee State University in Nashville.
1973	Oprah begins work at local television station WTVF in Nashville.
1976	Oprah gets a job at major television station WJZ in Baltimore, Maryland.
1978	Oprah begins cohosting *People Are Talking* on WJZ.
January 2, 1984	Oprah's first *A.M. Chicago* show airs.
December 18, 1985	*The Color Purple*, with Oprah costarring as Sofia, opens.

September 8, 1986	*The Oprah Winfrey Show* airs on 138 stations across the nation.
1987	Oprah opens Harpo Productions, becoming the first African-American woman to own a production studio.
1988	Harpo Productions buys *The Oprah Winfrey Show*.
February 1989	Oprah opens a restaurant called the Eccentric.
November 1991	Oprah speaks to the U.S. Senate about the National Child Protection Act, which became law two years later.
September 1996	Oprah's Book Club begins.
September 1997	Oprah's Angel Network begins.
1998	Oprah receives an Emmy Award for Lifetime Achievement; acts in and coproduces *Beloved*.
November 1999	Oprah awarded the National Book Foundation's 50th Anniversary Gold Medal.
1999	Oprah announces her involvement in the Oxygen Channel and *O: The Oprah Magazine*.
April 2000	The first issue of Oprah's magazine comes out.

SOURCES

Adler, Bill, ed. *The Uncommon Wisdom of Oprah Winfrey: A Portrait in Her Own Words.* Secaucus, NJ: Citadel Stars/Carol Publishing, 1997.

Calio, Jim. "If You Knew Oprah Like I Know Oprah..." *Redbook.* February 1998.

Canedy, Dana. "Oprah Winfrey and Hearst to Start Magazine." *The New York Times.* July 9, 1999.

Carter, Bill. "3 Female Executives Plan to Create Cable Channel for Women." *The New York Times.* November 24, 1998.

Causley, Janet. "The 50 Most Famous People of the Century." *Biography Magazine.* December 1999.

Chin, Paula and Cheakalos, Christina. "Touched by an Oprah." *People.* December 20, 1999.

Gates, Anita. "Unstoppable Oprah." *McCall's.* February 2000.

Levine, Ellen. "Winners of the Most Admired Women Poll." *Good Housekeeping.* January 1999.

Mair, George. *Oprah Winfrey: The Real Story.* Secaucus, NJ: Citadel Stars/Carol Publishing, 1998.

Noden, Merrell. *Oprah Winfrey.* New York: People Profiles/Time Life, Inc., 1999.

O'Neill, Anne-Marie. "Altered States." *People*. November 2, 1998.

"Oprah Winfrey." An A&E Biography. Aired January 16, 2000.

"Oprah Winfrey." *People*. December 28–January 4, 1999.

"Oprah Winfrey's Commencement Address, Wellesley College." May 30, 1997. Downloaded from http://www.wellesley.edu/Public Affairs/Commencement/1997/winfrey.html on 8/7/99

"Oprah Winfrey Reveals the Real Reason Why She Stayed on TV." *Jet*. November 24, 1997.

Powell, Joanna. "Oprah's Awakening." *Good Housekeeping*. December 1998.

"Quotation of the Day." *The New York Times*. February 27, 1998.

Russell, Lisa and Dampier, Cindy. "Oprah Winfrey." *People*. March 15–22, 1999.

Smoron, Paige. "All the Oprah You Could Want." *Chicago Sun-Times*. April 18, 2000.

Tannen, Deborah. "The TV Host: Oprah Winfrey." *Time*. June 8, 1998.

Verhovek, Sam Howe. "Talk of the Town: Burgers vs. Oprah." *The New York Times*. January 21, 1998.

"What's the Beef, Oprah?" *Time* for Kids. February 13, 1998.

"Winfrey Venture Gets an Editor." *The New York Times*. August 26, 1999.

To learn more about Oprah and the organizations she supports, visit these Internet sites:

www.Oprah.com — the official Oprah Web site
www.marwen.org — Web site for Marwen
www.habitat.org — Web site for Habitat for Humanity
www.joinaad.org — Web site for Athletes Against Drugs

I N D E X

ABOUT THE AUTHOR

Tanya Lee Stone is a former editor of children's books who now writes full-time. She is the author of more than a dozen books, including *Rosie O'Donnell: America's Favorite Grownup Kid* and *Diana: Princess of the People.*

In addition to her writing, Tanya runs Project Angel Food, an organization that she founded in 1997. Project Angel Food gathers food that will be thrown out by supermarkets and restaurants and delivers it to shelters and community centers.

She lives in Burlington, Vermont, with her husband, Alan, and her son, Jacob.